Epilepsy in Dogs

John Sanders, MA

Editor in Chief: Alaya Grace, CVT

Printed in the United States of America

ISBN **978-1467969819**

Contents:

Introduction: What is Epilepsy in Dogs?

Epilepsy in dogs results in fits and is due to a defect in the brain itself. In some breeds it can be passed through the generations and can be common, particularly in dog families. In some dog breeds, most significantly the German Shepherd, epilepsy is inherited and is most frequently seen in males. Occasionally epilepsy is the results of minor damages to the brain due to a blow to the head or due to oxygen starvation in a tough birth.

Epilepsy tends to start in dogs between one and five years old. If your pet is outside this age range then it is rather more likely that they are afflicted with a different disease.

The German Shepherd Dog, or Alsatian, is one breed affected by epilepsy.

Some dogs appear to know when they're about to have an epileptic fit. They may exhibit certain behaviors such as circling or hiding under a chair. These signs are usually very individual to the dog.

A seizure is not the same as a "heart spell". A heart spell, or possibly a faint from a weak heart ,causes an animal to collapse abruptly, usually using a yelp and then your pet will lie quietly. The heart may possibly pound and also the tongue may go blue. They might not breathe for a couple of seconds. There may possibly be loss of control of the bladder. A fit or seizure typically includes some type of muscle twitching. The eyelids may possibly flick, as well as the legs and body twitching. Animals will also collapse into a seizure, but usually not with a yelp. They may lose bladder control and from time to time bite their tongues. The breathing is often rough and intermittent and also the tongue may also go blue.

Once the fit starts your dog will appear to be comatose - they won't be able to hear or make a response to you. Often they may yelp – during the fit --or lose control over their bladder or bowels. Most episodes last between one and three minutes. After an episode dogs also tend to behave in individual ways. Your pet may have a set pattern of behavior that they follow after each fit - as an example asking to go outside or finding a quiet corner to lay in.

Typically epilepsy start several years after the damage has occurred, so it isn't always easy to make a connection between the two separate events.

Taking Care of Your Epileptic Pet

Recognizing the Type of Seizure

There are two basic types of seizures: Grand mal and Petit Mal.

Grand Mal

Usually a complete seizure where your pet loses consciousness, accompanied by bladder and bowel problems. Legs, entire body and eyes twitch. There may perhaps be breathing difficulties; the tongue may typically go blue. If it goes on too long, the brain may perhaps come to be deprived of oxygen and your pet can die. In most circumstances, even so, seizures last between thirty seconds and two minutes and the dog will come out from the seizure on their own. Before the seizure takes place, animals could be in a pre-ictal or prodromal state which you could see as confused or abnormal behavior right up until the seizure starts. When a seizure is over, animals are normally exhausted and extremely disorientated.

Partial or "Petit Mal"

These seizures are mini seizures which may well or might not progress into complete seizures. Animals are completely mindful of what is occurring, but their legs, faces and bodies may possibly twitch and they may shed the capacity to use their limbs correctly. They will normally try to crawl to their owners for comfort for the duration of the seizure, which again, normally lasts only a brief time.

What to Do During an Episode

You might like to make notes or, if you happen to have a camera, take a picture to show to your vet. A good description will help your vet decide if your pet has an episode or is falling down for some other reason. When your dog starts a fit take a note of the time it starts and the time it ends.

Other than making sure your dog isn't able to harm himself (for instance placing a pillow under his head if he is on a hard surface), you shouldn't interfere with a dog that is having a fit. Never attempt to put your hand within his mouth in an episode or you're likely to get bitten.

If your dog comes out of the episode inside five minutes then permit him time to recover silently before contacting your vet. It is much better for your dog to recover silently at home instead of being forced into the automobile and carried off to the animal hospital immediately. It is mostly not feasible to remove the reason behind the episodes or cure the disease – for example, the damage to the brain has already been done -- so your vet will use medicine to regulate the fits.

If your pet doesn't come out of a seizure this is known as "Status Epilepticus" and it can be an emergency. You must administer an anti epileptic drug, such as Valium (Diazepam) or your vet may need to give your pet a general anesthetic to end the seizing. Some individuals with epileptic pets are permitted to help keep injectable Valium or Valium tablets at home. In case you have the injectable Valium, you may either inject it in to the muscle (ask your vet to show you how), or squirt it up their nose or into the rectum, in which it will likely be absorbed.

Episodes could cause damage to the brain and if your dog has repeated episodes these make it rather more likely that further episodes will happen. They may bite their tongue and there may seem to be lots of blood but is not likely to be major; your dog won't swallow its tongue.

Taking Your Pet to the Vet

When your vet first inspects your dog, they won't know whether your dog has epilepsy or another condition. It is not likely that your vet will see your dog in an episode so it's important that you're able to describe in detail what occurs. Your vet may have to run an entire range of tests to make certain that there's no other basis for the fits. These include blood tests, most likely X-rays, and your vet may even suggest an MRI of your dog's brain.

It's critical to realize this treatment won't cure the illness but just manage the signs - even a well-controlled epileptic will have occasional episodes.

General Care Tips

You have to have patience when handling an epileptic pet. The drugs used to treat epilepsy regularly don't stop the episodes altogether, but will make them less frequent. Once your pet begins treatment it's probable this will need to be continued for the remainder of their life. Treatment must be continued regularly and at approximately the same time each day.

If the medication is stopped all of a sudden it may result in a fit. It generally takes one or two months to get the drug dosage just correct for your dog.

It's very rare that your epileptic pet will stop having fits altogether. Medication may control the episodes in order that they don't influence your dog's way of life however, if you stopped treatment the episodes would come back. Nevertheless -- your dog should receive regular checkups at your vet to make certain the drugs aren't causing any complications, there's a good likelihood that your dog will live a full and content life. Most dogs with epilepsy can be controlled by drugs which are given each day by mouth.

Medications:

Valium

Diazepam is applied as a short-term remedy of seizures in dogs and short-term and long-term remedy of seizures in cats. For emergent remedy of seizures, the regular dose is 0.5cmg/kg intravenously, or 1-2cmg/kg on the injectable solution administered in the rectum.

Valium is a drug of the Benzodiazepine sedative class. Valium (diazepam) acts on the limbic, thalmic and hypothalmic regions from the central nervous process to potentiate the results of inhibitory neurotransmitters, raising the seizure threshold within the motor cortex.

Precise suggestions for each dog need to be made by the attending veterinarian, but normally, dogs that have had one particular single seizure aren't provided valium treatment.

Dogs that possess a history of clustering (have over 1 seizure in 24 hours) or dogs who lapse into standing (either a continuous seizure lasting at least five minutes, or two or more separate seizures with no clear recovery in involving every single seizure) would be candidates for the rectal and oral Valium protocol.

When applying rectal Valium to quit cluster seizures, it's very important that the rectal Valium be administered all through or just right after the first seizure. It can be nearly impossible to stop seizures with valium immediately after 2 or 3 seizures have occurred. Use the proper dose of rectal Valium quickly following the 1st Grand Mal.

The key to an effective remedy would be to administer another dose on the anti-convulsant medicine when they've recovered sufficient to safely swallow. Preserve the anti-seizure level in the bloodstream by administering oral Valium 20 minutes immediately after dosing with rectal Valium and then continue dosing the oral Valium just about every one to two hours for the next 12 to 36 hours or for the time frame the cluster seizures have occurred within the past.

By preserving the anti-seizure effect of oral Valium within the bloodstream, many owners have had good results with getting rid of or at least substantially decreasing any further seizures.

Valium may perhaps lead to drowsiness, incoordination or disorientation. However these indicators are also typical in canines straight away just after a seizure. These unwanted effects are temporary. Valium is amongst the safer anti-seizure drugs that are definitely used, due to the fact it is actually metabolized really quickly. This means that even when as well a great deal is administered the unwanted effects are not going to last extended because the drug is eliminated so rapidly from the physique.

How to give rectal Valium

Either your vet or the pharmacy should have offered or sold you a syringe big sufficient to hold the quantity determined to be right for one dose for you dog, with the accompanying needle to draw the valium into the syringe. You may also require a teat cannula, a 'Tom Cat Catheter' or perhaps a regular catheter which will fit the syringe you might have been offered right after the needle has been removed. If you are given a common catheter, the tubing length must be cut down to about six inches. Measure from the major cut in the bottom. Immediately after cutting, mark the tubing three inches from the end with a permanent ink form marker. The 3 inches of tubing is the component that goes to the rectum.

For liquid Valium in a brown bottle meant for injection: With the needle attached to the syringe, pull the plunger back and fill the syringe with air equal for the cc's of liquid valium you will be giving.

Insert the needle to the opening within the bottle, making certain the needle tip is just prior to the rubber guard on the bottle.

Push the plunger on the syringe, placing the air from the syringe to the bottle. This aids to create a vacuum within the bottle.

Turn the bottle and also the needle upside down. Now the bottle is on top, and the needle beneath, then the syringe, with the entire plunger toward the floor. Pull the plunger back out to the proper cc dosage marking; the valium should now fill the syringe.

When the proper quantity of valium is inside the syringe, take out the syringe in the needle and attach the catheter.

Spread KY Jelly or Vaseline around the rectum for

lubrication. Attach the syringe towards the other end with the catheter. Insert three inches from the catheter into the rectum and push the plunger, gradually and steadily.

Phenobarbital

As well as being used on a day-to-day basis to stop fits, Phenobarbital is often used to stop episodes in progress.

Phenobarbital's top action happens four to eight hours after you give your pet the tablet. While the drug isn't FDA accepted for use in dogs, its use is accepted in veterinary practice. The drug is available in tablet or liquid form. You can get the drug from a vet and from a pharmacy with a prescription. When Phenobarbital treatment begins, it takes one or two weeks to achieve a stable blood level. Till that time has passed, it probably won't stop the fits. Contact your vet if your dog has more than one fit every fortnight or the episodes go on longer than 5 minutes.

The drug comes in grams or grains. In mg, Phenobarbital comes in fifteen mg, thirty mg, sixty mg or one hundred mg pills. Makers who use grains offer one / eight grain (eight mg), 0.25 grain (sixteen mg), 0.5 grain (32 mg) or one grain (sixty five mg).

Because assimilation, speed of metabolism and distribution can differ from pet to pet, printed dose suggestions only function as a general guide. Your vet will likely adjust this dose based mostly on blood levels, fit activity and complications of the medicine.

Your vet will inform you how frequently to give your pet their medication. As a rule, phenobarbital is given each twelve hours and will be given as near to each twelve hours to avoid episodes. Usually a single trough level is picked up just before a dose is administered. Once a control level is attained, serum levels in the blood should be tested every six months. Most critically, liver enzymes GGT, ALT and Alkaline Phosphatase ought to be checked each 3 or 4 months to observe liver function.

The best test of whether your pet is receiving the right dose is whether your pet still has episodes. Having only 1 fit a month is regarded as good control.

Drug Activity

Phenobarbital holds back episodes by lowering neural activity. This effect doesn't just affect the neurons connected with epilepsy -- it affects other neurons too. Lots of the complications of this drug spring from this neural effect. These complications can include sleepiness, disproportionate urination, unwarranted thirst or hunger, excitability or restlessness, loss of coordination, and hind end weakness. Many of these side-effects reduce or vanish after the initial few weeks of treatment. Long term complications tend to be excessive urination, thirst and hunger.

Side Effects

Prolonged or long-term use of Phenobarbital can end up with liver scarring and liver failure in a tiny proportion of animals. Caught sufficiently early, these problems can be reversed with a straightforward diet change, and the slow decrease or elimination of the drug. Also recommended is the addition of SamE, Denosyl or milk thistle to the diet.

These liver tests are used because they will be able to indicate the start of a difficulty in time to switch medicine and take suitable action. Bile acid testing every six months can supply an earlier appearance of an issue so that corrections can be made before it is much too late. General loss of appetite, weight reduction and protracted erratic diarrhea and vomiting are common warning signs. While a rise in drinking and urinating can also signal liver issues, these are common with Phenobarbital and it could be tough to tell the difference.

If your dog has developed liver illness, the reduction in medication can be by as much as twenty-five percent a week. Some vets suggest a decreasing of ten percent each week or so. The major problem with dropping drug treatment is fit recurrence, which is most inclined to occur during withdrawal or inside a few months of stopping treatment. Phenobarbital speeds up liver activity and, if used with other medicines that are routinely broken down by the liver, may make them be processed more swiftly, so requiring them to be given at a higher dose.

Potassium Bromide (KBr)

Potassium bromide (KBr) is the drug that
veterinarians would usually recommend when it comes to
treating epileptic dogs with liver disease. As early as 1857,
people suffering from epilepsy had already been treated with
potassium bromide; however, nowadays, this drug is quickly
being recognized in its effectiveness in handling canine
epilepsy. Epileptic dogs with kidney complications are treated
with sodium bromide. Some dogs have been found to have a
negative response to phenobarbitol or primidone, so a
combination of phenobarbitol and potassium bromide or
sodium bromide is recommended in these cases.

After adding potassium bromide to the therapy of 10
dogs acting as test subjects to a recently concluded study, the
canines' phenobarbitol-induced seizures showed significantly
improved control. The tendency to cluster and the severity of
the said seizures also showed a substantial decline. Professor
Dorothea Schwartz-Porsche (Sisson/LeCouteur) conducted a
study prior to the aforementioned one. The study showed
that the addition of potassium bromide to phenobarbitol or
primidone received a positive response from 5 of 9 epileptics
who experienced complications with phenobarbitol alone.
Initially unaided by phenobarbital, seizure control in 83% of
dogs improved through bromide therapy, with 26% of the

83% dogs being entirely free of seizures, Podell and Fenner report.

Since bromide is not commercially available, veterinarians currently acquire the drug from chemical supply houses. Bromide is not yet approved for use in dogs. It is dissolved in water and added to the dog's food as an American Chemical Society reagent. Release forms are signed and safety precautions are given to the dog owner before availing of the said drug. According to Thomas, in order to free veterinarians from having to formulate the said drug, there are custom pharmacies that produce bromide in capsules or suspension.

Bromide is to be handled with care, because bromide toxicity or bromism can cause several side effects, namely uncoordination, depression, lethargy and muscle pain. For humans taking KBr, there are no known dermatological or gastrointestinal complications.

Zonisamide

In recent studies, Zonisamide, which is an anticonvulsant licensed for man in the US in 2000, was found effective in its therapeutic use for dogs suffering from refractory epilepsy. Aside from the occurrence of some hepatic metabolism, most of the drug is excreted without significant change in the urine of dogs after an estimated half life of 15 hours (Matsumoto et al 1983, Thomas 2003).

Other than possibly reducing the release of presynaptic glutamate release (Mac Donald 2002), zonisamide can also block voltage-dependent sodium and calcium channels. It is also reported that the dopamine and serotonin levels in striatal and hippocampal structures increase with zonisamide (Kaneko et al 1993, Okada et al 1995).

Although zonisamide appears to be safe and with limited side-effects when used in dogs, several reports conclude that mild ataxia and sedation is possible at the start of the treatment. Dogs have also suffered from vomiting and appetite loss with the use of the drug (Dewey et al, 2004). The recommended dose rate is a target serum concentration of 10-40 ug/ml, implying a 5 to 10 mg/kg BID. Minor changes in blood count and a spike in liver weight are some of the observations in a study conducted (Walker et al 1988) after using a dose of 75 mg/kg body weight, which is four times the recommended dose. A study was done with rats, describing an induction of tolerance possibly caused by kindling phenomenon (increase of severity of the epileptic process) or an induction of functional tolerance (Hamada et al 2001).

When it comes to canine epilepsy and the use of zonisamide as anticonvulsant treatment, not much data is available (Dewey et al 2004, Boothe et al 2005, Saito et al 2005). Von Klopmann and others conducted a study in 2007 providing an evaluation of zonisamide and its effectiveness as an add-on to the usual anticonvulsant therapy of refractory epilepsy in dogs. This study gives refractory epilepsy the following definition: a lack of adequate response to treatments of phenobarbitol and/or potassium bromide despite therapeutic serum levels of one or both of the said drugs. A dosage of 10mg/kg body weight BID PO of zonisamide was administered as add-on therapy (Matsumo et al 1983, Walker et al 1988, Boothe et al 2005, Saito et al 2005). Following the administration of the drug and the measurement of serum concentrations, serum samples were collected from the dogs in the study at various time intervals, resulting in a zonisamide reference ranging from 10 to 40 μ/ml (Matsumoto et al 1983, Walker et al 1988).

Succeeding the start of zonisamide therapy through ataxia and sedation, six dog owners noticed mild side-effects caused by the sulphonamide-based anticonvulsant drug. It is important that clinicians are aware of the possible side-effects of the drug that are likened to complications caused by sulphonamides.

The administration of zonisamide was found to decrease the frequency, severity and duration of seizures of most dogs. This indicates that zonisamide is beneficial in refractory cases, given the response of a high number of dogs experiencing at least a 50% decrease in seizure frequency. Seven dogs experienced good seizure control, leading to a reduction of previous anticonvulsant therapy (phenobarbitol, potassium bromide). This was done without a resulting impairment of seizure control. The drug was even said to have caused a reduction in side effects and a better quality of living in several animals. When the dose of conventional anticonvulsants was reduced for one Border collie, there was a reduction of sedation allowing normal behavior, typical of the dog's breed, to manifest once again.

Siezure control was negatively affected after an initial positive response in a subgroup of responder dogs. This change in effectiveness is common for several drugs, as well as zonisamide in rats (Hamada et al 2001).

Zonisamide is not available in several countries and is not widely used because of its high cost. A generic formulation is available in the United States, though no published studies exist regarding the use of this active ingredient in dogs.

Further evaluation of the "honeymoon effect" caused by functional tolerance in zonisamide add-on therapy, as well as the effectiveness of zonisamide as monotherapy, is in order.

Keppra (Levetiracetam)

In 1999, the United States Food and Drug Administration approved Levetiracetam (Keppra) for its anti-seizure effects. Though it is not completely understood how levetiracetam works against seizures, it is classified differently from other anti-seizure drugs. It is known to be well-tolerated by humans with few known side-effects.

Levetiracetam is orally administered to dogs and is not bound to protein. After an estimated elimination half-life of 3.3 hours (in dogs – it normally lasts 7.7 hours in people), the drug is excreted through the urine with low liver metabolism. Minimal negative effects, despite increased doses, were shown in laboratory dogs after several safety studies (UCB Pharma, Inc. Data on file).

As far as evaluations in using levetiracetam for the idiopathic epilepsy of dogs, there are no published studies. However, a clinical trial of levetiracetam in dogs with idiopathic epilepsy (uncontrolled through phenobarbitol and bromide) is being conducted by a couple of veterinary schools.

Gabapentin

A recently completed study conducted by U.K. clinicians included 11 dogs with refractory idiopathic epilepsy showing generalized tonic-clonic seizures. It studied the effectiveness of Gabapentin (already used in human epileptics refractory to the combination of phenobarbitol and potassium bormide) as add-on therapy for the managing refractory epilepsy in dogs. The drug is recommended for administration every 6 hours, but it was shown to be effective even with a dose of thrice daily. The elimination half-life is estimated to be 3-4 hours in dogs, and contrary to how it is for humans, gabapentin is metabolized by the liver in dogs. Though still undocumented, this causes a risk of hepatotoxicity in dogs, even more so when the drug is administered with phenobarbitol. In this study, with success measured from a 50% reduction in seizure frequency, 45% of the 11 dogs demonstrated better seizure control.

The underlying causes of the idiopathic epilepsy the dogs were suffering from were investigated through CSF tap and MRI brain exams. A combination of phenobarbitol and KBr were administered to all of the dogs, who had therapeutic serum concentrations of these drugs. A starting dose of 10 mg/kg q 8 hours were received by each dog for at least three months.

Of the 11 dogs, the seizure frequency of five dogs lessened by 50% per week. There were, however, several days when many of the dogs exhibited cluster seizure activity. Generally speaking, gabapentin was well-tolerated with five dogs showing ataxia and sedation as side effects, while after 18 months, one dog developed sterile panniculitis (after termination of gabapentin treatment, this was soon resolved).

In conclusion, based on this study, gabapentin can cause the reduction of seizure frequency in some dogs with refractory idiopathic epilepsy. To verify and further evaluate these results, a larger study on the potential benefits of gabapentin in treating epileptic dogs is warranted.

Felbamate

Felbamate is being used for the treatment of epilepsy and seizures in dogs. It is one of the relatively new anticonvulsant drugs and one of the advantages of its use is that it can normally be combined with phenobarbitol and/or potassium bromide without causing additional sedation. The drug hasn't yet been used extensively; thus, though it initially appears to be safe for use in dogs, some still debate about its efficacy and contend that its use should be monitored regularly with blood testing. It is prescribed by some veterinarians that liver enzymes be checked at least every two or three months, while others trust that the drug is safe. They contend that the monitoring of liver enzymes in the blood is wholly unnecessary.

The side-effects caused by felbamate aren't yet complete, since it has only been used recently in treating dogs. The complete implications of these side-effects, including frequency and severity, are also still not fully explored. Currently, the known side-effects of felbamate are as follows: vomiting, sedation and nausea in dogs. For people, felbamate has been found to cause a serious blood disease involving the red blood sells (aplastic anemia) and death of the liver cells (hepatic necrosis). It is important to note these side-effects in humans as the drug may also cause problems to dogs that receive it.

Treatment of cats suffering from seizures and/or epilepsy using felbamate is still widely considered as unsafe and not recommended by most veterinarians.

Genetics and Inheritability

According to Dr. Anita Oberbauer—professor at the University of California, Davis Department of Animal Science— dogs are "the most genetically engineered species on the planet" due to a long history of breeding dogs for desirable traits and breeding out undesirable characteristics.

Many years ago, when I was living in the United Kingdom, I bred working Siberian Huskies. I had a basic understanding of genetics—enough to know that when I wanted to breed all-white Siberians into my line, that I had to find a sire and a dam with the recessive and elusive white gene and breed them together. A few months later, my bitch produced a litter of six puppies: three grey and white, two black and white, and one white. This was a result of a little knowledge, and a lot of good luck. Why "luck"? Choosing a sire and dam that carry those traits was nothing more than an educated guess; it isn't possible to tell what genes a dog has just by looking at it. A dog breeder must look at pedigrees and use the laws of probability to breed a trait in, or breed one out.

Not being able to "see" genes are part of the reason why it's difficult to breed out diseases from an affected population. You can't tell what dogs are carriers for the disease by looking at them, and there's no DNA test (at time of writing) that will tell you which dogs are carriers. However, a basic understanding of genetics and probabilities could prevent a lot of heartache in the future. At a minimum, sires and dams that have produced litters of pups with a known genetic disorder should not be bred from again unless the breeder is certain which parent has the gene for the disease.

A Standard Poodle breeder friend of mine, "Maggie" bred two of her dogs together and produced six beautiful, healthy puppies. Because the puppies were so perfect, she decided to go for another litter with the same sire and dam a year later. Just before the second litter was born, the first phone call came in from one of the owners of a bitch from the first litter with the bad news: her puppy had just been diagnosed with Addison's disease. Within the next few weeks, three out of six puppies came down with the disease. Maggie was distraught, but informed all of the new owners of the likelihood of Addison's in their new puppies. Within two years, four out of the litter of six puppies came down with Addison's disease.

How inheritability works

Every cell in the body contains DNA, or deoxyribonucleic acid. DNA is made up of repeating pieces of information located on nucleotide bases. The sections of DNA that give instructions on how to make and operate a living organism are called genes. The genes are located in compacted sections of DNA called chromosomes. Dogs have over 20,000 genes and 38 pairs of chromosomes in each cell (Oberbauer & Bell, n.d.).

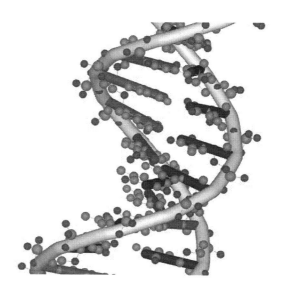

Double helix DNA structure. One section of DNA, like the one depicted here, can be thought of as a gene.

Each pair of non-sex chromosomes is called an autosome. Because autosomes come in pairs, each gene has two possible states, called alleles. Alleles can be identical (homozygous) or different (heterozygous).

The chromosome(s) responsible for diseases are always found at the same location —for example in

Portuguese water dogs, the loci associated with late onset
Addison's disease is always chromosomes CFA12 and 37. [1]

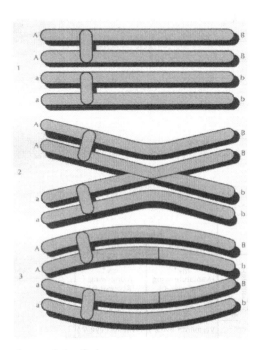

A model of chromosomes.

When a hereditary trait is referred to as dominant, it
means that if an allele has a certain characteristic (i.e. short
legs), it will show up no matter what the other paired allele is
coded for. According to Adam Miklósi, author of the book
Dog Behavior, evolution and cognition, short legs in dogs is

<hr />

[1] See Chase et. al, 2006

actually a genetic abnormality called achondroplasia, where the legs stop growing during puppyhood. Because short legs are a dominant trait (like brown eyes in humans), a long-legged dog and a short-legged dog can be bred together to result in a short-legged dog every time. By mating dogs together in this way, the abnormaility becomes "fixed" in certain dog populations. This resulted in the dachshunds and Chihuahuas of today.

On the other hand, a recessive trait means that in order for the trait to appear, two alleles must be exactly the same. An example of a recessive trait is blue eyes in Siberian huskies—in order for the trait to show through, both alleles must carry the chromosome for blue eye color.

A third type of trait is also possible, called incomplete dominance, where the trait may or may not show through. For example, spots on a dog's coat is an example of incomplete dominance. A dog many have heavy spotting, no spotting, or if they are a heterozygous individual (i.e. one allele is dominant and the other is recessive), they might have mild spotting.

The heritability of a trait is designated with a number from 0 to 1. The designation '0' means that there is no probability of inheriting the trait for a population and that the trait is entirely environmental. Spoken language in humans is an example of a trait that is environmental (heritability=0) as is a cropped tail in dogs (for the uninitiated, tail docking is performed by people—it is not inherited).[2] A designation of 1 means that there is 100% certainty the trait will show up if the affected allele is present in a population. Blood type is an example of a trait that is inherited (heritability=1). Dr. Anita Oberbauer (2006) reports that for Portuguese Water Dogs, Addison's disease has an inheritability of 0.49 (+/- 0.16). Dr. Oberbauer's research also suggests that Addison's is most likely due to a recessive mode of inheritance (i.e. two identical alleles are needed for the disease to manifest) and the more inbred an animal is, the higher the likelihood of Addison's; highly inbred dogs in the study had up to a 25% chance of being affected with Addison's disease. Research is continuing in many breeds under CGAP as Dr. Oberbauer's team continues to work on discovering the location of the affected genes on the chromosomes.

It stands to reason that there are genes responsible for certain diseases and eventually those genes will be

---

[2] **Dogs' tail docking has actually been banned in the UK since 2007 by the Animal Welfare Act.**

identified, enabling dog breeder's to take steps to eradicate the inheritability of particular disease in dogs.

Related Diseases

Canine Epileptoid Cramping Syndrome (CECS), also called Spike's disease, is usually a hereditary canine illness with similarities to epilepsy, and it is generally related with Border Terriers. CECS is actually a recently acknowledged difficulty which is theorized as being a metabolic, neurological or muscle disorder. The cause has not however been identified.

In 1996, a Dutch Border Terrier owner, Joke Miedema acquired a puppy named Roughmoor Blue Spike (identified as Spike). About a year later, Spike began exhibiting strange symptoms, starting with obvious absentness and some staggering. Four years later, Spike started showing serious signs and symptoms like cramping and epileptic-like fits; tests carried out at Utrecht University in 2002 showed the dog did not have epilepsy.

In 1997, Giana Plange, a German vet and Border Terrier breeder started getting calls from people that owned dogs bred by her, reporting epileptic-like signs and symptoms. Plange looked at more than a hundred Border Terriers, eventually figuring out that the condition was quite possibly hereditary. Other researchers started to be concerned, and quite a few Border Terriers lines in Britain and the USA are suspected as carriers.

By the end of 2001, Spike had 2-3 epileptoid episodes per week. Owners of cramping dogs started to connect through Net groups, which includes a help group started by Miedema. The condition came to become known as "Spike's Illness."

By the spring of 2003, Plange gave the situation the title Canine Epileptoid Cramping Syndrome.

Breed lines of suspected carriers began to be documented; and the initial identifiable sufferer was dated to 1974.

Cause

As of 2008, the inheritance mode has not been identified.

Signs and symptoms:

- borborygmus
- intestinal cramping
- dizzines
- exaggerated stretching
- muscle contractions
- staggering
- trembling
- unusually slow or methodical walking

Dogs usually continue to be alert and responsive in the course of episodes that can last anywhere from seconds to minutes. In some dogs, one or two episodes are observed followed by long-term or even permanent remission. In other dogs, episodes may well be frequent or progressive in nature.

Treatment

There is certainly presently no recognized cure for CECS, but some owners have had achievement with drug and diet program therapies.

Drugs

Diazepam and Clorazepate Dipotassium happens to be used efficiently to stop cramping in some scenarios, but it has failed to assist in other circumstances. Scopolamine (Buscopan) suppositories or injections and Gaviscon helps with the stomach problems.

Diet

Some owners have had varying levels of success with dietary alterations. A gluten-free and/or raw diet program may help, or staying away from:

- Artificial colors
- Artificial flavors
- Beef
- corn
- dairy
- eggs
- rice
- soy

Commercial hypoallergenic formula feeds may help.

Research

Analysis is at this time currently being carried out to uncover the genetic basis of CECS; to develop a diagnostic check or tests; and to search out cures or remedies. Scientific studies are being held at the University of Utrecht, and in the University of Missouri's Canine Epilepsy Network.

Cheaper Treatment Options

If your dog has **epilepsy**, you might experience sticker shock at the veterinary office. However, it is possible to reduce the cost of treatment, or even get it for free!

    1.   Shop Around for Medications

If money is tight, do a little shopping around at veterinarians and reduced your monthly medicine cost.

    2.   Google is your friend, but don't expect miracles.

    3.   Try compounding pharmacies for cheap medications. Here are a few to consider:

Nora Apothecary (www.noraapothecary.com)

1 (800) 729-0276

Congaree Veterinary Pharmacy
(www.congareevetrx.com)

1 (877) 939-1335

Valley Drug and Compounding
(www.1pharmacy.com)

1 (818) 788-0635

Pet Pharm (www.petpharm.org)

Summit Chemist (www.svprx.ca) (in Canada)

1-866-794-7387

4. Find the cheapest vet around and give him your business: There's a well-known pet clinic in my home town called Herschel Animal clinic. They don't have the bells and whistles of the upscale veterinary practices (they rarely answer their phone and there's no brightly lit, cushy waiting room— sometimes you have to wait out in the parking lot for

an hour or two to be seen). But they are cheap, and for someone with a chronically ill **dog**, that can literally be a lifesaver.

5.   Cut down on the dosage of medication with your vet's help.

Finally, if you can't afford it, find a way to afford it: one reason that Dr. Plant at Herschel offers treatments at the lowest price possible is because he knows it's sometimes prohibitively expensive. One former client of his just didn't get the treatment for their dog, and the animal "just wasted away," he said. "It was sad, sad." Although there isn't a free pet clinic system in the states like there is in the UK (the PSDA), there are many routes you can try to obtain reduced cost, or even free, care.

- Write a letter to your vet: this will probably work if you've been a long term client and are likely to continue being a client in the future. Write a personal letter and tell him that you cannot afford full treatment costs. Tell him what you can afford a month. Ask him/her for their help. Remember that your vet will still have to purchase the drug at base cost, so don't expect miracles. But it's worth a shot (if you'll excuse the pun).

- Contact shelters and rescue organizations in your area and ask them if they know of any low cost clinics. One website—www.pets911.com, offers a search feature where you can enter your zip code and find local rescue and animal organizations that may be able to help.

- Consider finding another home for your pet. If you have a purebred animal, contact your nearest breed-specific rescue and tell them that you are having trouble affording medications. Some rescue organizations will allow you to advertise for a new home on their website, and someone who is familiar with your pet's disease might be willing to give your dog a home. You can also look for breed-specific rescue discussion boards—there are many on the web. Whatever you do, make sure that you don't give your animal to the local animal control or city-run shelter; they immediately euthanize sick animals.

- Make A Wish: if all else fails you can try posting for help on the Make a Wish page at www.wishuponahero.com. They match donors to people with needs. You never know when an angel (maybe a local vet?) will offer a helping hand!

[50]

Acknowledgments

Rendering of DNA picture by Ghutchis @ Flickr.com

Chromosomes by A Journey Around My Skull @ Flickr.com

References

Bowen R.. Glucocorticoids. Article posted on website Colorado State University. Retrieved August 1, 2009 from: http://www.vivo.colostate.edu/hbooks/pathphys/endocrine/adrenal/gluco.html may 26, 2006.

Case, L. The Dog: Its Behavior, Nutrition and Health. 2nd ed. Hoboken, NJ: Wiley-Blackwell. 2005.

Chase K, Sargan D, Miller K, Ostrander E, Lark K. Understanding the genetics of autoimmune disease: two loci that regulate late onset Addison's disease in Portuguese Water Dogs. Int J Immunogenet. 2006 Jun;33(3):179-84.

Davidson G, and. Plumb D. Ketoconazole. Veterinary drug handbook-client edition. Article posted on website Aboretum View Animal Hospital. Retrieved aug 13, 2009 from http://avah.org/pdf/systemic/Ketoconazole.pdf

Forney B. Prednisone for veterinary use. Article posted on website Wedgewood Pharmacy. Retrieved August 1, 2009 from: http://www.wedgewoodpharmacy.com

Hughes A, Nelson R, Famula T, Bannasch D. Clinical features and heritability of hypoadrenocorticism in Nova Scotia Duck Tolling Retrievers: 25 cases (1994–2006) JAVMA, Vol 231, No. 3, August 1, 2007

Oberbauer A. Genetic evaluation of Addison's disease in the Portuguese Water Dog. BMC Vet Res - 01-JAN-2006; 2: 15

Oberbauer A. & Bell D, Genetics Primer. Article posted on website Tualatin Kennel Club. Retrieved August 19, 2009 from:

http://www.tualatinkc.org/pdf/Genetics%20Primer.
pdf

Oberbauer A, Benemann K, Belanger J,
Wagner D, Ward J, Famula T, Inheritance of
hypoadrenocorticism in Bearded Collies AJVR, Vol
63, No. 5, May 2002

OSU Boren Veterinary Medical Teaching
Hospital. Oklahoma State University College for
Veterinary Sciences. Retrieved July 20, 2009 from
http://www. http://www.cvhs.okstate.edu

Richards M Corticosteriod side effects. Article
posted on website Vet Info. Retrieved august 9, 2009
from: http://www.vetinfo.com/ceffect.html

Tilley L, Goodwin J. Manual of Canine and
Feline Cardiology. Philadelphia, Pennsylvania:
Saunders. 3 edition (January 15, 2001)

Wikipedia: CECS. Article Retrieved
November 11, 2011.
http://en.wikipedia.org/wiki/Canine_Epileptoid_Cra
mping_Syndrome

Your Own Vet: Epilepsyhttp://yourownvet.com/?tag=animal-health-epilepsy-and-fits

WB Thomas, DVS. Epilesy. Article Retrieve d November 5, 2011. http://www.canine-epilepsy-guardian-angels.com/OralandRectalProtocol.htm